CALVIN ON SCRIPTURE AND DIVINE SOVEREIGNTY

OTHER RELATED SGCB TITLES

Calvinism in History by Nathaniel McFetridge

Calvin Memorial Addresses by Orr, Warfield etc

The Humanness of John Calvin by Richard Stauffer

The Word and Prayer: Classic Devotions by John Calvin

CALVIN
ON SCRIPTURE
AND DIVINE SOVEREIGNTY

JOHN MURRAY

SOLID GROUND CHRISTIAN BOOKS
BIRMINGHAM, ALABAMA USA

Solid Ground Christian Books
PO Box 660132
Vestavia Hills AL 35266
205-443-0311
sgcb@charter.net
solid-ground-books.com

Calvin on Scripture and Divine Sovereignty
by John Murray (1898 – 1975)

First Solid Ground Edition May 2009

Special thanks to John Muether for all his help on this
project, including the indices.

This project has been completed in partnership with
the Committee for the Historian of the Orthodox
Presbyterian Church.

ISBN: 978-159925-203-2

Foreword to New Edition

In the vast sea of theological literature that has been produced over the ages, the lion's share disappears into an abyss of anonymity. People may have at one time read a book, but with the passing of time forget about it. Many books are written for the moment and therefore lack abiding significance. The same cannot be said for this little gem written by the late John Murray (1898-1975), professor of systematic theology at Westminster Theological Seminary in Philadelphia, Pennsylvania. Professor Murray was well known for his careful exegetically based systematic theology courses. Former students fondly recall that their favorite part of Professor Murray's courses was to work through the Hebrew or Greek text and listen to Murray expound the doctrines that grew organically from his exegetical spadework. However, as biblically grounded as Murray's teaching and theological writing were, he was not ignorant of the history of doctrine. The present volume is a testimony of Murray's intimate familiarity with one of the Reformed church's theological giants, John Calvin (1509-64).

In these lectures from 1959 Professor Murray addresses three key issues concerning Calvin's theology: the doctrine of Scripture, its authority, and the sovereignty of God. Written in the looming shadow of Karl Barth (1886-1968), one of the most influential theologians of the twentieth century, Murray challenged Barth's attempt to co-opt Calvin for the cause of neo-orthodoxy. Barth claimed that Calvin was a forerunner of his own distinct departure from the Reformed tradition by arguing that subsequent Reformed theology deviated from the paradigm set by the Genevan giant.

Murray meticulously showed through his careful survey of Calvin's writings that Calvin was no Barthian. Calvin did not merely affirm the infallibility of Scripture, the divine certainty that the Scriptures were effectual to the ends that God had purposed in the salvation of sinful man. To assert the infallibility of Scripture and not its inerrancy – that it was without error in matters of science and history – was not an option for Calvin. Murray explained that these twin teachings are both entailed in Calvin's view of Scripture's authority. In a similar way, Murray recovered Calvin's view of divine sovereignty, something that Barth had significantly re-structured until it looked nothing like Calvin's teaching, let alone the apostle Paul's.

What commends the republication of these lectures is that Murray addresses subjects of perennial inquiry. Even at present there are well-intended but nonetheless mistaken theologians from within the confessional Reformed church who have argued that inerrancy is a post-Reformation development driven by rationalism. Murray's study is a most welcome antidote to such false claims. Anyone interested in a brief but well informed survey of Calvin's theology on these key subjects do well to consider Professor Murray's little book.

J. V. Fesko
March 2009

Preface

The three lectures, here reproduced in slightly revised form, were given under the auspices of the Reformed Fellowship, Inc. in Grand Rapids, Michigan on May 21, 22, 26, 1959 in connection with the commemoration of the four hundred and fiftieth anniversary of the birth of John Calvin and the four hundredth anniversary of the publication of the definitive edition of *The Institutes of the Christian Religion.*

I wish to express my deep gratitude to the Reformed Fellowship, Inc. for the invitation to deliver these lectures and for all the courtesies extended to me during my stay in Grand Rapids while these lectures were being delivered.

I make grateful acknowledgment to the Columbia University Press, New York, for permission to quote from Edward A. Dowey, Jr.: *The Knowledge of God in Calvin's Theology* (1952) and to the Wm. B. Eerdmans Publishing Company, Grand Rapids, to quote from *ed.* John F. Walvoord: *Inspiration and Interpretation* (1957).

To the Reformed Fellowship, Inc. I extend my warm thanks for undertaking to publish these lectures in book form.

JOHN MURRAY

Philadelphia
June 12, 1959

Foreword

The three chapters of this book have their origin in a series of lectures on certain aspects of Calvin's theology, delivered by John Murray, professor of Systematic Theology at Westminster Theological Seminary, Philadelphia. These lectures were given in the Eastern Avenue Christian Reformed Church of Grand Rapids, Michigan, before large audiences of ministers, professors, students, and interested laymen. The occasion was the 450th anniversary of the birth of John Calvin and the 400th anniversary of the appearance of the final edition of Calvin's immortal work, *The Institutes of the Christian Religion*.

Three of the four lectures mentioned above are included in this volume. They deal respectively with the teaching of Calvin on the Inspiration of the Scriptures, the Authority of the Scriptures, and the Sovereignty of God.

The commemorative character of the occasion for these lectures, the prevailing keen interest in the subject of the inspiration and infallibility of the Bible, and the fact that Professor Murray is regarded by many as the foremost among living Reformed theologians in America, as well as his thorough acquaintance with Calvin's works, combine to lend special significance to the publication of this material.

The lectures which this book embodies were delivered and are published under the auspices of the Reformed Fellowship, Inc., publishers of the magazine, *Torch and Trumpet*.

REFORMED FELLOWSHIP, INC.
Grand Rapids, Michigan

Contents

Chapter I
Calvin's Doctrine of Scripture

Chapter I

Calvin's Doctrine of Scripture

The contention that Calvin's view of the inspiration of Scripture was not the high doctrine of plenary, verbal inspiration, espoused by the Reformed dogmaticians of the seventeenth century, has emanated from many quarters. It is noteworthy that within the last few years this question has received from students of Calvin thorough and exacting treatment. It is gratifying that the two studies which this present decade has produced and which have brought the most painstaking research to bear on the question have reached the same conclusion that in Calvin's esteem the original Scriptures were inerrant. In the words of E. A. Dowey: "There is no hint anywhere in Calvin's writings that the original text contained any flaws at all."[1] "The important thing to realize is that according to Calvin the Scriptures were so given that—whether by 'literal' or 'figurative' dictation—the result was a series of documents errorless in their original form."[2] And Kenneth S. Kantzer, even more recently, has written that the evidence in support of the view that Calvin held to the "rigidly orthodox verbal type of inspiration....is so transparent that any endeavor to clarify his position seems almost to be a work of supererogation."[3] "The merest glance at Calvin's commentaries," he adds, "will demonstrate how seriously the Reformer applied his rigid doctrine of verbal inerrancy to his exegesis

---

[1] Edward A. Dowey, Jr.: *The Knowledge of God in Calvin's Theology*, New York, 1952, p. 100.

[2] *Ibid.*, pp. 101f.

[3] Ed. John F. Walvoord: *Inspiration and Interpretation*, Grand Rapids, 1957, p. 137.

of Scripture" and Kantzer claims that "attempts to discover a looser view of inspiration in Calvin's teaching fall flat upon examination."[4]

Kantzer is to be complimented on his decision not to regard the task of providing the evidence in support of the foregoing conclusions a work of supererogation. He has furnished us with what is perhaps the most complete induction of the evidence drawn from the wide range of Calvin's works. And, since it was not a superfluous undertaking for Dr. Kantzer, it is perhaps not without necessity that we should devote some attention to the same question on this memorial occasion.

The present writer is not disposed to regard the question, as it pertains to Calvin's position, with any such attitude as might be described as cavalier. There are passages in Calvin that cannot be dismissed with a wave of the hand. It is significant that the passages which, in my judgment, occasion the most acute difficulty are precisely those which so able a controversialist as Charles A. Briggs has been wise enough to appeal to in support of his own contention that Calvin did not maintain biblical inerrancy.[5] It is well to place these in the forefront for two reasons. First, it is in the interest of fairness in polemics not to suppress what constitutes the strongest argument in support of an opposing position. Second, it is a principle of hermeneutics to interpret more difficult passages in the light of the more perspicuous, a principle that applies to the interpretation of theologians as well as of Scripture.

The passages in mind are Calvin's comments on Matthew 27:9; Acts 7:14-16; Hebrews 11:21. The first is concerned with the reference to Zechariah 11:13, attributed to Jeremiah, and Calvin comments: "How the name of Jeremiah crept in, I confess that I do not know, nor do I anxiously concern myself with it. The passage itself clearly shows that the name of Jeremiah was put down by mistake for that of

---

[4]*Ibid.*, pp. 142f.
[5]Charles Augustus Briggs: *The Bible the Church and the Reason*, New York, 1892, pp. 219ff.; *cf.* pp. 110ff.

Zechariah (11:13), for in Jeremiah we find nothing of this sort, nor any thing that even approaches to it."[6]

The second passage deals with the question of the number of souls reported by Stephen to have gone down into Egypt with Jacob and with the statement that Abraham bought a sepulchre of the sons of Hemor rather than of Ephron the Hittite, as Genesis 23:8-18 informs us. Calvin's remarks are: "Whereas he saith that Jacob came into Egypt with seventy-five souls, it agreeth not with the words of Moses; for Moses maketh mention of seventy only. Jerome thinketh that Luke setteth not down, word for word, those things which Stephen had spoken, or that he took this number out of the Greek translation of Moses (Gen. xlvi. 27), either because he himself, being a proselyte, had not the knowledge of the Hebrew tongue, or because he would grant the Gentiles this, who used to read it thus. Furthermore, it is uncertain whether the Greek interpreters set down this number of set purpose, or whether it crop (crept) in afterward through negligence, (mistake;) which (I mean the latter) might well be, forasmuch as the Grecians used to set down their numbers in letters. Augustine, in his 26th book of *City of God*, [*De Civitate Dei,*] thinketh that Joseph's nephews and kinsmen are comprehended in this number; and so he thinketh that the words *went down* doth signify all that time which Jacob lived. But that conjecture can by no means be received. For, in the mean space, the other patriarchs also had many children born to them. This seemeth to me a thing like to be true, that the Seventy Interpreters did translate that truly which was in Moses. And we cannot say that they were deceived; forasmuch as (in) Deut. x., where this number is repeated, they agree with Moses, at least as that place was read without all doubt in the time of Jerome; for those copies which are printed at

---

[6]*Commentarius in Harmoniam Evangelicam, ad* Matt. 27:9. Able expositors have found in Matt. 27:9 an allusion to Jeremiah, chapters 18 and 19: *cf.* E. W. Hengstenberg: *Christology of the Old Testament*, E.T., Vol. IV, Edinburgh, 1865, pp. 40ff. Hence it need not be maintained, as Calvin alleges, that the name Jeremiah is here a textual error. As will be shown later, the mistake to which Calvin here refers is, in his esteem, one of textual corruption and not one on Matthew's part.

this day have it otherwise. Therefore, I think that this difference came through the error of the writers which wrote out
the books (*librariorum,* copyist). And it was a matter of no
such weight, for which Luke ought to have troubled the
Gentiles which were accustomed with the Greek reading. And
it may be that he himself did put down the true number; and
that some man did correct the same amiss out of that place
of Moses. For we know that those which had the New Testament in hand were ignorant of the Hebrew tongue, yet skilful
in the Greek.

"Therefore, to the end (that) the words of Stephen might
agree with the place of Moses, it is to be thought that that
false number which was found in the Greek translation of
Genesis was by them put in also in this place; concerning
which, if any man contend more stubbornly, let us suffer him
to be wise without measure. Let us remember that it is not
without cause that Paul doth forbid us to be too curious
about genealogies.........."[7]

In regard to verse 16 Calvin writes: "And whereas he saith
afterward, they were laid in the sepulchre which Abraham
had bought of the sons of Hemor, it is manifest that there is
a fault (mistake) in the word Abraham. For Abraham had
bought a double cave of Ephron the Hittite (Gen. xxiii. 9),
to bury his wife Sarah in; but Joseph was buried in another
place, to wit, in the field which his father Jacob had bought
of the sons of Hemor for an hundred lambs. Wherefore this
place must be amended."[8]

The third passage (Heb. 11:21) is concerned with the
discrepancy between the two statements that Jacob worshipped
on the top of his bed and that he worshipped on the top of
his staff. The difficulty in itself is by no means acute.[9] But
Calvin's statement at this point is the one with which we

---

[7]*Commentarius in Acta Apostolorum ad* Acts 7:14; E.T. by Henry
Beveridge, Grand Rapids, 1949, Vol. I, pp. 263f.

[8]*Ibid., ad* Acts 7:16.

[9]The question turns on the difference of vowels attached to the same
Hebrew consonants. If certain vowels are supplied, the term means "bed,"
if others, "staff." There is good ground for the latter alternative, following
certain versions and Heb. 11:21.

are concerned. "And we know," he says, "that the Apostles were not so scrupulous in this respect, as not to accommodate themselves to the unlearned, who had as yet need of milk; and in this there is no danger, provided readers are ever brought back to the pure and original text of Scripture. But, in reality, the difference is but little; for the main thing was, that Jacob worshipped, which was an evidence of his gratitude. He was therefore led by faith to submit himself to his son."[10] The disturbing remark in this quotation is that "the Apostles were not so scrupulous in this respect, as not to accommodate themselves to the unlearned, who had as yet need of milk." For in this instance Calvin is not reflecting upon some error that might have crept in in the course of copying the text of Hebrews 11:21 but upon the practice of the inspired writers themselves to the effect that they were not concerned with precise accuracy in a detail of this kind. If this is Calvin's thought, then we might say that, in his esteem, an error of historical detail is compatible with the canons which governed the inspired writers and therefore compatible with the inspiration under which they wrote. As far as I am aware, this remark constitutes the most formidable difficulty in the way of the thesis that Calvin believed in biblical inerrancy. We are not, however, in a position properly to interpret and evaluate this statement and the others quoted above until we have made a broader survey of Calvin's teaching.

Calvin's greatest work *The Institutes of the Christian Religion* is interspersed with pronouncements respecting the character of Scripture and we should be overlooking some of the most relevant evidence if we did not take account of them.

"Whether God revealed himself to the fathers by oracles and visions, or, by the instrumentality and ministry of men, suggested what they were to hand down to posterity, there cannot be a doubt that the certainty of what he taught them was firmly engraven on their hearts, so that they felt assured and knew that the things which they learnt came forth from

---

[10]*Commentarius in Epistolam ad Hebraeos, ad* 11:21; E.T. by John Owen, Grand Rapids, 1948, p. 291.

God, who invariably accompanied his word with a sure testimony, infinitely superior to mere opinion."[11] This quotation is of interest because it is concerned with the certification accorded to men who were the recipients of revelation by other modes of revelation than that of Scripture, a certification by which certitude of the truth was engraven on their hearts. This quotation also prepares us for what Calvin regarded as providing the necessity for inscripturation. So we read in the next paragraph, "For if we reflect how prone the human mind is to lapse into forgetfulness of God, how readily inclined to every kind of error, how bent every now and then on devising new and fictitious religions, it will be easy to understand how necessary it was to make such a depository of doctrine as would secure it from either perishing by the neglect, vanishing away amid the errors, or being corrupted by the presumptuous audacity of men" (I, vi, 3). It is the liability to error, associated with tradition, that makes inscripturation necessary, and the *documentation* of the "heavenly doctrine" (*coelestis doctrina*) guards it against the neglect, error, and audacity of men.

We shall have occasion to give examples later on from Calvin's other works of his characteristic dictum that the Scripture speaks to us with a veracity and authority equal to that of God speaking to us directly from heaven. We do not read far into the *Institutes* before we come across the most explicit affirmation to this effect. "When that which professes to be the Word of God is acknowledged to be so, no person, unless devoid of common sense and the feelings of a man, will have the desperate hardihood to refuse credit to the speaker. But since no daily oracles are given from heaven, and the Scriptures alone exist as the means by which God has been pleased to consign his truth to perpetual remembrance, the full authority which they obtain with the faithful proceeds from no other

---

[11]In quoting from the *Institutes* and *Commentaries* in the remaining part of this lecture, I have made use of the various translations. But I have often given my own rendering when I deemed it necessary to depart from the renderings of other translators. I believe these translations of mine are more pointed and accurate in reference to the subjects being discussed.

consideration than that they are persuaded that they proceeded from heaven, as if God had been heard giving utterance to them" (I, vii, 1).

It is in this same context that Calvin speaks of the Scriptures as the "eternal and inviolable truth of God." It is in this same brief chapter that the following propositions are plainly asserted. God is the author of the Scriptures. The Scriptures themselves manifest the plainest signs that God is the speaker (*manifesta signa loquentis Dei*). This is the proof that its doctrine is heavenly. We are never established in the faith of this doctrine until we are indubitably persuaded that God is its author (I, vii, 4 *passim*). And so he adds: "Being illuminated therefore by him [*i.e.*, the Spirit], we no longer believe, either on our own judgment or that of others, that Scripture is from God, but, in a way that surpasses human judgment, we are perfectly assured ... that it has come to us by the ministry of men from the very mouth of God" (I, vii, 5—*ab ipsissimo Dei ore ad nos fluxisse*). "We feel the firmest conviction that we hold an invincible truth" (*idem*). "Between the apostles and their successors, however, there is, as I have stated, this difference that the apostles were the certain and authentic amanuenses of the Holy Spirit and therefore their writings are to be received as the oracles of God, but others have no other office than to teach what is revealed and deposited in the holy Scriptures" (IV, viii, 9). At this stage it is not necessary to quote further from the *Institutes,* for in these few quotations there is virtually all that can be derived from that source. It is when we turn to other sources that the implications of these statements are brought into clearer focus.

With reference to Calvin's concept of inspiration and of its effects we should expect that no passages would offer him the opportunity to express his thought more pointedly than II Timothy 3:16 and II Peter 1:20. In this expectation we are not disappointed. In reference to the former he says: "First, he (Paul) commends the Scripture on account of its authority; and, secondly, on account of the utility that springs from it. In order to uphold the authority of the Scripture, he declares that it is divinely inspired (*Divinitus inspiratam*); for, if it be so, it is beyond all controversy that men ought to receive it with reverence. This is a principle which distinguishes our religion from all others, that we know that God hath spoken to us, and are fully convinced that the prophets did not speak at their own suggestion (*non ex suo sensu loquutos esse*) but that they were organs of the Holy Spirit to utter only those things which had been commanded from heaven. Whoever then wishes to profit in the Scriptures, let him, first of all, lay down this as a settled point, that the law and the prophecies are not a doctrine delivered by the will of men, but dictated (*dictatam*) by the Holy Spirit.... Moses and the Prophets did not utter at random what we have from their hand, but, since they spoke by divine impulse, they confidently and fearlessly testified, as was actually the case, that it was the mouth of the Lord that spoke (*os Domini loquutum esse*).... This is the first clause, that we owe to the Scripture the same reverence which we owe to God, because it has proceeded from him alone, and has nothing of man mixed with it" (*nec quicquam humani habet admixtum*).

In his comments on II Peter 1:20 he again reminds us that the prophecies are the indubitable oracles of God and did not flow from the private suggestion of men and therefore we must be convinced that God speaks to us in the Scripture. And so he continues: "the beginning of right knowledge is to give that credit to the holy prophets which is due to God.... He says that they were moved, not that they were bereaved of mind ... but because they dared not to announce anything of themselves (*a se ipsis*) and only obediently followed the Spirit as their leader, who ruled in their mouth as in his own sanctuary."

Before making remarks respecting the import of these assessments of the origin, authority, and character of Scripture, it may not be amiss to cull from other places a few quotations to elucidate and confirm these statements of his. With reference to Mark as the author of the Second Gospel he says: "Mark is generally supposed to have been the private friend and disciple of Peter. It is even believed that he wrote the

Gospel as it was dictated to him by Peter, so that he merely performed the office of amanuensis or scribe. But on this subject we need not give ourselves much trouble, for it is of little importance to us, provided we hold that he is a properly qualified and divinely ordained witness who put down nothing except by the direction and dictation of the Holy Spirit."[12] Respecting the four Evangelists he says that God "therefore dictated to the four Evangelists what they should write, so that, while each had his own part assigned to him, the whole might be collected into one body."[13] On Romans 15:4 Calvin paraphrases Paul's thought by saying: "there is nothing in Scripture which is not useful for your instruction, and for the direction of your life" and then adds: "This is an interesting passage, by which we understand there is nothing vain and unprofitable contained in the oracles of God.... Whatever then is delivered in Scripture we ought to strive to learn; for it would be a reproach offered to the Holy Spirit to think that he has taught us anything which it does not concern us to know; let us then know that whatever is taught us conduces to the advancement of piety."[14]

A great deal has been written in support of the thesis that the Bible is infallible in matters that pertain to faith and life, to the doctrine of salvation and the kingdom of God, but not in other matters concerned with history or science. And the teaching of Calvin has been appealed to in support of this distinction. Perhaps you will permit a quotation from one of the ablest and most eloquent of the protagonists of this contention, Charles Augustus Briggs. He writes: "It is well known that Calvin and Luther and other reformers recognized errors in the Scriptures.... But what do these errors amount to, after all? They are only in minor matters, in things which lie entirely beyond the range of faith and practice. They have nothing to do with your religion, your faith in God and His Christ, your salvation, your life and

---

[12]"Argumentum in Evangelium Jesu Christi secundum Matthaeum, Marcum, et Lucam."
[13]"Argumentum in Evangelium Ioannis."
[14]*Comm. ad* Rom. 15:4.

conduct.... The Scriptures are pure, holy, errorless, so far
as their own purpose of grace is concerned, as the only infallible rule of the holy religion, the holy doctrine, and the
holy life. They are altogether perfect in those divine things
that come from heaven to constitute the divine kingdom on
earth, which, with patient, quiet, peaceful, but irresistible
might, goes forth from the holy centre through all the radii
of the circle of human affairs and persists until it transforms
the earth and man."[15] It is this distinction which Briggs
alleges to be implicit in Calvin's position, and his contention
is to the effect that the infallibility predicated of Scripture is,
therefore, for Calvin, consistent with the errors, which, he
alleges, Calvin admits. But it is not only Dr. Briggs who makes
this kind of allegation. No one has been a more painstaking
student of Calvin than Emile Doumergue. On the question of
inspiration he has performed the service of exposing the
fallacy of R. Seeberg's contention that Calvin taught mechan-
ical dictation. But Doumergue also maintains that Calvin
did not teach literal, verbal inspiration and that for Calvin
the important thing was not the words but "the doctrine, the
spiritual doctrine, the substance."[16]

Here we are brought to the crux of the question. Does
Calvin's position on inspiration fall into line with that
espoused and defended by Dr. Briggs? Is it true that Calvin
did not consider the words important but only the spiritual
doctrine? It is this thesis that I am compelled on the basis
of the evidence to controvert. In dealing with the question
we shall have to take account of several considerations.

1. It is true that Calvin lays great stress, as we found in
the quotations from his works, upon the heavenly doctrine of
which Scripture is the depository. It is the liability to corruption on the part of men that made necessary the inscripturation of the heavenly doctrine. Thereby it is guarded against
the neglect, error, and audacity of men. But that there is in

---

[15]*Op. cit.*, pp. 112, 115, 116.
[16]E. Doumergue: *Jean Calvin: Les hommes et les choses de son temps*,
Tom. IV, Lausanne, 1910, p. 78. Doumergue's discussion, referred to in
these pages, is found in the tome cited above in pp. 70-82.

Calvin the kind of alleged distinction between the heavenly doctrine and the Scripture in which that heavenly doctrine is deposited is a thesis which his own statements do not bear out. He affirms most explicitly that the Scripture is from God, that it has come to us from the very mouth of God, and that in believing the Scripture we feel the firmest conviction that we hold an invincible truth. To insinuate that this conviction has respect simply to the heavenly doctrine, as distinct from Scripture as the depository, is to interject a distinction of which there is no suggestion in the relevant passages. In other words, Calvin identifies the doctrine of which he speaks with the Scripture itself. "The Law and the Prophecies are not a doctrine delivered by the will of men, but dictated by the Holy Spirit,"[17] and this is the settled point, he insists, that must be laid down if we are to profit in the Scriptures. And the emphasis is pervasive that we owe to the Scripture the same reverence we owe to God.

2. To say the least, it would be mystifyingly strange that Calvin would have affirmed so expressly that the writers of Scripture "did not utter at random what we have from their hand," that Scripture "has nothing of man mixed with it," that the writers "fearlessly testified that it was the mouth of the Lord that spoke" and that the Holy Spirit "ruled in their mouth as in his own sanctuary,"[18] if his conception of inspiration did not apply to the details of words and to what we might call random statements. For Calvin, there are no random statements in Scripture because the writers did not speak at random but always by divine impulse. And, furthermore, we must remember that he has warned us against the impiety of thinking that there is anything unprofitable or vain in the Scripture; the Holy Spirit has taught us everything in the Scripture it concerns us to know, and all that is taught conduces to the advancement of piety.

3. When we examine the evidence which Doumergue adduces in support of his allegations that Calvin has not taught

---

[17]*Comm. ad* II Tim. 3:16.
[18]*Cf.* citations given above.

verbal inspiration, it is nothing short of exasperating to find
how destitute of relevance this supposed evidence is. Under
one caption Doumergue says, "Words have been added or
suppressed"[19] and then proceeds to cite instances. He appeals
to Calvin's comments on Eph. 2:5; Heb. 9:1; I Tim. 1:3;
James 4:7. Let us see then what Calvin says at these points.

At Eph. 2:5 Calvin comments, with reference to the words
"by grace ye are saved," as follows: "I know not whether some
one else inserted this, but, as there is nothing alien to the
context, I freely accept it as written by Paul."[20] It is quite
apparent that Calvin is here reflecting simply on the question
as to the possibility of addition in the course of transcription.
His own judgment is that these words are Pauline and proceeds
to expound their import on this assumption. In short, his
judgment is that they were not added. This is clearly a question of the proper text and nothing more. It has absolutely
nothing to do with the question at issue.

At Heb. 9:1 Calvin says: "Some copies read 'first tabernacle':
but I think there is a mistake in the word 'tabernacle,' nor do
I doubt but that some unlearned reader, not finding a noun
for the adjective, and in his ignorance applying to the tabernacle what had been said of the covenant, unwisely added
the word 'tabernacle.' "[21] Again, this is purely a matter of what
Calvin regards as textual corruption by an unlearned reader
and to him alone belongs the error, not at all to the writer
of Hebrews. In fact, why does Calvin esteem this to be the
work of an unlearned reader? Precisely because he is jealous
for the accuracy of the original author. If Calvin were, as
Doumergue alleges, not concerned about words but about the
spiritual doctrine, he would not have bothered to reflect on
the folly of the unlearned reader but would have been ready
to attribute what he regarded as an error to the writer of
Scripture itself.

On I Tim. 1:3 Calvin says: "Either the syntax is elliptical,
or the particle *hina* is redundant; and in either case the mean-

---

[19]*Op. cit.*, p. 76.
[20]*Comm. ad* Eph. 2:5.
[21]*Comm. ad* Heb. 9:1.

ing will be clear."[22] This is concerned solely with the question of style. An ellipsis is simply an abbreviated manner of speech in which something plainly understood is not expressed and redundancy is simply a manner of speech by which something is expressed which is not indispensable to the meaning.

On James 4:7 we read: "Many copies have introduced here the following sentence: 'Wherefore he saith, God resisteth the proud, but giveth grace to the humble.' But in others it is not found. Erasmus suspects that it was first a note in the margin, and afterwards crept into the text. It may have been so, though it is not unsuitable to the passage."[23] Surely no comment is necessary to show the irrelevance to Doumergue's allegation.

Another caption under which Doumergue derives support for his thesis is that "there are differences,"[24] meaning, of course, that there are differences between the biblical writers when dealing with the same subjects, and cites Calvin's comments on Matt. 8:27; Matt. 9:18. That Calvin recognises the differences in the accounts given by the various evangelists we should fully expect. Who with even a modicum of understanding does not observe these differences? But that these differences constitute any evidence of the lack of verbal inspiration or any such judgment on Calvin's part is precisely what Calvin is most jealous to deny. On Matt. 9:18 he says: "Those who imagine that the narrative, which is here given by Mark and Luke, is different from that of Matthew, are so clearly refuted by the passage itself, that there is no necessity for a lengthened debate. All the three agree in saying that Christ was requested by a ruler of the Synagogue to enter his house for the purpose of curing his daughter. The only difference is, that the name of Jairus, which is withheld by Matthew, is mentioned by Mark and Luke; and that he represents the father as saying, 'My daughter is dead,' while the other two say that she was in her last moments, and that, while he was bringing Christ, her death was announced to him on the

---

[22]*Comm. ad* I Tim. 1:3.
[23]*Comm. ad* James 4:7.
[24]*Op. cit.*, p. 77.

road. But there is no absurdity in saying that Matthew, studying brevity, merely glances at those particulars which the other two give in minute detail. But since all the other points agree with such exactness, since so many circumstances conspire as to give it the appearance of three fingers stretched out at the same time to point out a single object, there is no argument that would justify us in dividing this history into various dates. The Evangelists agree in relating, that while Christ, at the request of a ruler of the synagogue, was coming to his house, a woman on the road was secretly cured of a bloody flux by touching his cloak; and that afterwards Christ came into the ruler's house, and raised a dead young woman to life. There is no necessity, I think, for circuitous language to prove that all the three relate the same event. Let us now come to details."[25] Calvin's own statement on this very subject we may quote again. "He (God) therefore dictated to the four evangelists what they should write, in such a manner that, while each had his own part assigned him, the whole might be collected into one body; and it is our duty now to blend the four by a mutual relation, so that we may permit ourselves to be taught by all of them, as by one mouth."[26]

Again Doumergue appeals to the fact that "the order of time is not always observed"[27] and instances Calvin's comments on Luke 4:5 and Matt. 27:51. We all know that the Evangelists do not always follow a chronological arrangement of their narratives and, of course, Calvin does also. But this is a question of literary form and not of verbal inspiration.

Finally, in connection with Doumergue's contention that for Calvin the words were not important but the "spiritual doctrine," it is Calvin's treatment of quotations from the Old Testament in the New that Doumergue relies on chiefly in this connection.[28] He appeals to Calvin's comments on the use made by New Testament writers, particularly Paul, of

[25]*Comm. in Harmoniam Evangelicam, ad* Matt. 9:18; E.T. by William Pringle, Grand Rapids, 1949, Vol. I, pp. 409f.
[26]"Argumentum in Evangelium Ioannis."
[27]*Op. cit.,* p. 77.
[28]*Op. cit.,* pp. 78f.

Old Testament passages. In this connection a distinction must be appreciated. Calvin recognizes, of course, as every one must perceive, that the New Testament writers, in referring to the Old Testament, did not always quote the Old Testament passages verbatim. And Calvin is fully aware of the difficulty that sometimes confronts us in the use made of Old Testament passages. For example, he says with respect to Rom. 10:6: "This passage is such as may not a little disturb the reader, and for two reasons. It seems to be improperly twisted by Paul and the words themselves turned to a different meaning."[29] And on Rom. 11:8 he thinks that the words quoted from Isaiah are "somewhat altered" and that Paul does not here "record what we find in the prophet, but only collects from him this sentiment that they were imbued by God with the spirit of maliciousness so that they continued dull in seeing and hearing."[30] And again on Eph. 4:8 he says: "To serve the purpose of his argument, Paul has departed not a little from the true sense of this quotation" (*testimonium*).[31] On the same text with reference to the clause "and gave gifts to men," he adds: "There is rather more difficulty in this clause; for the words of the psalm are, 'thou hast received gifts for men,' while the apostle changes this expression into 'gave gifts' and thus appears to exhibit an opposite meaning."

But the all-important point to be observed is that Calvin in each case goes on to justify the apostle and to show that what appears to be an unwarranted change is one perfectly compatible with the designed use of the passage in each case, a use furthermore in perfect consonance with the inspiration under which the apostle wrote. With reference to the apparently improper use of Deut. 30:12 in Rom. 10:6, Calvin continues: "This knot may be thus untied" and then proceeds to give what he considers to be the necessary resolution of the difficulty. In like manner on Rom. 11:8 he maintains that there is no discrepancy between what Paul elicits from the

[29] *Comm. ad* Rom. 10:6.
[30] *Comm. ad* Rom. 11:8.
[31] *Comm. ad* Eph. 4:8.

word of the prophet and what the prophet himself said but that rather "Paul penetrates to the very fountain." And although on Eph. 4:8 he admits that Paul "deviated not a little from the true meaning" of the Old Testament passage, yet he launches immediately into a defense of the apostle against the charge of having made "an unfair use of Scripture" and protests that "careful examination of the Psalm will convince any reader that the words, 'he ascended up on high,' are applied strictly to God alone." Finally, with reference to the change from "received" to "gave" in the same text, he says: "Still there is no absurdity here; for Paul does not always quote the exact words of Scripture, but, after referring to the passage, satisfies himself with conveying the substance of it in his own language." In this case, however, Calvin thinks that when Paul says "gave gifts to men" he is not intending to quote Scripture at all but uses his own expression adapted to the occasion.

We are compelled, therefore, to draw the following conclusions. (1) When Calvin recognizes that Paul, for example, does not always quote the Old Testament verbatim, he is as far as possible from insinuating that the actual words of the Old Testament were not important. And he is likewise not insinuating to the least extent that the precise and original meaning of the Old Testament passages, as indicated by their exact terms, was not important. He is not even remotely suggesting an antithesis between the "substance" which the apostle elicits from the Old Testament text and the text of the Old Testament itself, as if the former were important and the latter not. (2) There is not the remotest suggestion that the precise terms used by the apostle in the use of the Old Testament (terms which may deviate from the precise terms of the Old Testament) are unimportant. Indeed, the opposite is the case. It is exactly because Calvin was concerned with the precise terms and words used by the apostle that he entered upon the discussion and resolution of the difference between the terms in the Old Testament and in Paul's use of the same. In reality the only inference to be drawn from these discussions on the part of Calvin, and particularly from the resolution which he offers in each case, is that in his esteem words and terms were of the greatest importance. (3) What Calvin says is that Paul, in quoting from the Old Testament in these instances, elicited from the passage what was appropriate to his purpose at the time. He does not say or imply that for Paul the exact terms and import of the Old Testament passage were unimportant, but simply that it was sufficient for the apostle to derive from the Scripture concerned the particular truth or application relevant to the subject in hand. And, for Calvin, both are important as providing us with the whole truth, the truth expressed in the Old Testament and that enunciated in Paul's interpretation and application. The whole belongs to the spiritual doctrine which the Scripture conveys to us.

In these passages, therefore, there is no warrant for Doumergue's allegation that for Calvin the words were not important but only the spiritual doctrine or substance. This sets up a contrast which Calvin does not entertain and it is a contrast which Calvin's own express declarations do not tolerate.

4. A great deal of scorn has been heaped for the last seven decades upon what has been called the modern "dogma of the inerrancy of the original autographs" and upon the "modern scholastics who have generated this dogma."[32] This question of the autographs and of the mistakes that have crept in in the course of transmission introduces us to a most important phase of the evidence bearing upon Calvin's view of Scripture. We have had occasion to quote several passages from Calvin in which he reflected upon these mistakes of copyists and, in one case, upon the blunder of an unlearned reader. It is not necessary to review these passages. It is sufficient to be reminded that Calvin discusses this matter of the proper text of a particular passage and registers his judgment for the very purpose of ascertaining what was the text penned by the original writer, whether it be Luke or Paul or the writer of the epistle to the Hebrews. Calvin was greatly concerned to ascertain what this text was whenever

---

[32]C. A. Briggs: *op. cit.*, p. 97; *cf.* pp. 98, 114.

there was occasion to raise any question respecting it. Of this there is copious evidence. Now why this concern? Obviously because he was jealous to be sure of the autographic text. And is it not this jealousy that lies behind the whole science of textual criticism? Scholars differ in their judgments on particular problems. But they all have interest in getting back to the autographic text. Hence the premise of centuries of labor on this question is the importance of the autographic text.

But in the case of Calvin there was much more at stake than the abstract question of the text of the original author. We have found that his interest is also concerned with the question of veracity. He rejects a certain reading in Hebrews 9:1, for example, because that reading would not comport with the facts of the case as he construed them. He attributes the reading to an ignorant reader. Why such reflections? Surely because he is jealous not to attribute this reading to the writer of Hebrews. And that means that the assumption on which he proceeds is that the original writer could not be regarded as susceptible to such an error.

In reference to this interest on Calvin's part in the autographic text of Scripture our final observation must be that his jealousy for the original text cannot be dissociated from his estimate of Scripture as the oracles of God, that Scripture has nothing human mixed with it, and that in all its parts it is as if we heard the mouth of God speaking from heaven. Errors in scribal transmission Calvin fully recognizes. In some instances he pronounces decisive judgment as to the reason and source of these errors. It is apparent that this jealousy is dictated by his conviction that the penmen of the Scriptures were the amanuenses of the Holy Spirit and could not have perpetrated such mistakes. This is tantamount to nothing less than his interest in an inerrant autograph.

We may with this in view return to the passages quoted at the beginning of this lecture and which were passed over until we should survey Calvin's teaching as a whole. These are Calvin's remarks on Matt. 27:9; Acts 7:14-16; Heb. 11:21. On Matt. 27:9 he says that "the name of Jeremiah was put down by mistake for that of Zechariah." In view of what we have found, we cannot now suppose that, in Calvin's esteem, this mistake was the work of Matthew. And the term he uses earlier when he says "How the name of Jeremiah crept in, I confess that I do not know" is precisely the term Calvin uses with reference to errors that have crept into the text. There is, therefore, not the least warrant to suppose that Calvin is thinking of an error in the work of Matthew, and there is every warrant to judge the opposite. He is thinking of scribal error.

In reference to Acts 7:16 when he says that there is a fault, that is, *erratum,* in the name Abraham and concludes by saying, "Wherefore this place must be amended," analogy would not allow for any other interpretation than that he is thinking of an error in the course of transcription.

In Acts 7:14 the difficulty connected with the number 75 he likewise thinks may have arisen, in the first instance, "through the error of the copyists" of the Greek Old Testament. Here he also entertains the possibility that Luke put down the true number and that some man corrected the same out of the Greek Old Testament where the number 75 appears. Yet he thinks it also possible that Luke may have used the number 75 since it appeared in the Greek version with which readers would be familiar and that "it was a matter of no such weight for which Luke ought to have troubled the Gentiles who were accustomed to the Greek reading." This latter statement may be considered along with his comments on Heb. 11:21. They both fall into the same category.

With respect, then, to these two statements that the number of the souls who went down to Egypt was not a matter for which Luke should have troubled the Gentiles who were accustomed to the Greek reading and that the writer of Hebrews was not so scrupulous but that he could accommodate himself to the unlearned who had as yet need of milk, what are we to say? Some remarks may help to place the question in proper perspective.

1. Calvin does recognize that the writers of Scripture were not always meticulously precise on certain details such as

those of number and incident. And this means that the Holy Spirit, by whom, in Calvin's esteem, they wrote, was not always meticulously precise on such matters. It must be emphatically stated that the doctrine of biblical inerrancy for which the church has contended throughout history and, for which a great many of us still contend, is not based on the assumption that the criterion of meticulous precision in every detail of record or history is the indispensable canon of biblical infallibility. To erect such a canon is utterly artificial and arbitrary and is not one by which the inerrancy of Scripture is to be judged. It is easy for the opponents of inerrancy to set up such artificial criteria and then expose the Bible as full of errors. We shall have none of that, and neither will Calvin. The Bible is literature and the Holy Spirit was pleased to employ the literary forms of the original human writers in the milieu in which they wrote. If Solomon's temple took seven and a half years to build, as we can readily calculate (*cf.* I Kings 6:37, 38), are we to suppose that it is an error to say in the same context that Solomon was seven years in building it (I Kings 6:38)? Or if a certain king is said to have reigned twenty-two years (*cf.* I Kings 14:20), we must not impose upon such a statement the necessity of his having reigned precisely twenty-two years in terms of twenty-two times three hundred and sixty-five days.[33] He may have reigned only twenty-one years in terms of actual computation and yet twenty-two years in terms of the method of reckoning in use. The Scripture abounds in illustrations of the absence of the type of meticulous and pedantic precision which we might arbitrarily seek to impose as the criterion of infallibility. Every one should recognize that in accord with accepted forms of speech and custom a statement can be perfectly authentic and yet not pedantically precise. Scripture does not make itself absurd by furnishing us with pedantry.

2. We need not doubt that it was this distinction between the demands of pedantic precision, on the one hand, and adequate statement, that is, statement adequate to the situation

---

[33]For a discussion of such questions *cf.* Edwin R. Thiele: *The Mysterious Numbers of the Hebrew Kings*, Chicago, 1951.

and intent, on the other, that Calvin had in mind when he said that "the apostles were not so punctilious as not to accommodate themselves to the unlearned." We are not necessarily granting that Calvin's remarks are the best suited to the solution of the questions that arise in connection with Acts 7:14 and Heb. 11:21. We may even grant that the language used by Calvin in these connections is ill-advised and not in accord with Calvin's usual caution when reflecting on the divine origin and character of Scripture. But, if so, we should not be surprised if such a prolific writer as Calvin should on occasion drop remarks or even express positions inconsistent with the pervasive and governing tenor of his thinking and teaching. In Calvin we have a mass of perspicuous statement and of lengthened argument to the effect that Scripture is impregnable and inviolable, and it would be the resort of desperation to take a few random comments, wrench them from the total effect of Calvin's teaching, and build upon them a thesis which would run counter to his own repeated assertions respecting the inviolable character of Scripture as the oracles of God and as having nothing human mixed with it.

Chapter II

Calvin and the Authority of Scripture

Chapter II

Calvin and the Authority of Scripture

In the preceding lecture we have dealt with Calvin's doctrine of Scripture and have controverted the allegation that Calvin did not espouse a view of Scripture which would imply its inerrancy and verbal inspiration. In the situation in which we are placed today and more particularly in view of a good deal that has been written in comparatively recent years on Calvin's position in reference to Scripture, there would be a serious lacuna in our discussion if we did not reflect on other topics which are bound up with Calvin's teaching on the character of Scripture as the Word of God and with the interpretations of Calvin which have been advanced in reference to these topics.

One of these topics is that of the relation of Scripture to Christ as the Word incarnate. And this is pointedly stated as the relation of the written Word to the incarnate Word. Calvin leaves us in no doubt whatsoever that in his esteem the incarnate Son is the focal point of divine revelation. In the *Institutes* and the *Commentaries* the centrality of Christ is in the foreground. "The saints in former ages, therefore, had no other knowledge of God than what they obtained by beholding him in the Son as in a mirror. What I mean by this is that God never manifested himself to men than through his Son as his unique wisdom, light, and truth. From this fountain Adam, Noah, Abraham, Isaac, Jacob, and others drew all the knowledge they possessed of heavenly doctrine. From the same fountain all the prophets likewise drew whatever they taught of the celestial oracles."[1] Again, to quote another

---

[1]*Inst.*, IV, viii, 5.

example, he says: "For this reason Christ commands his disciples to believe in him, in order that they may distinctly
and perfectly believe in God. . . . For although, properly
speaking, faith ascends from Christ to the Father, nevertheless he indicates that, even though it were fixed on God,
it would soon disappear unless he interposed to give it stabil-
ity. . . . Wherefore although I accept that common saying
that God is the object of faith yet it needs some correction;
because it is not without reason that Christ is called the image
of the invisible God (Col. 1:15). By this appellation we are
advised that, unless God meets us in Christ, it is not possible
for us to have the knowledge that is unto salvation."[2] This
line of thought Calvin brings to a climax when he says that
the Turks in modern times "though they boast of having
the Creator of heaven and earth as their God, yet substitute
an idol in the place of the true God as long as they reject
Christ."[3] In view of this indispensable interposition and
mediation of Christ we should not be in the least surprised
to read early in the *Institutes,* in reference to Scripture itself:
"The letter, therefore, is dead and the law of the Lord slays
its readers wherever it is divorced from the grace of Christ
and only sounds in the ears without touching the heart."[4] "As
soon as we have gone out of Christ, we shall have nothing
else than the idols which we have formed, but in Christ
there is nothing but what is divine and what keeps us in
God."[5]

It is perfectly true, therefore, as Wilhelm Niesel says, that
Calvin "considers the word of the Bible as a dead and in-
effectual thing for us if it is not divinely vivified. . . and so
soon as it is separated from Him [Christ] it becomes a dead
body of letters without soul. Christ the soul of the law alone
can make it live."[6] "Jesus Christ is the soul of the law, the

---

[2]*Ibid.,* II, vi, 4.
[3]*Idem.*
[4]*Ibid.,* I, ix, 3.
[5]*Comm. ad* John 14:10.
[6]*The Theology of Calvin,* E.T. by Harold Knight, Philadelphia, 1956,
p. 32.

focal point of the whole of Holy Scripture."[7] But is this position regarding the centrality of the incarnate Word as the focal point of revelation in any way incompatible with the doctrine of verbal inspiration? This is what Niesel asserts. "When we hear Calvin assert so much we realize how misleading it is to regard him as the exponent of a literal theory of inspiration,"[8] and he affirms bluntly that Calvin for these reasons did not believe in the "inspired literal inerrancy" of Scripture. "Although he may incidentally speak of the divine inspiration of Holy Scripture, such remarks must in no case be interpreted to mean that Scripture as such is identical with the truth of God. No; the truth of God is Jesus Christ.... The teaching about literal inspiration leads to Bibliolatry and overlooks the fact that there is only one incarnation of the divine word, of which Holy Scripture is the witness."[9]

There are in particular two things to be said respecting this contention, a contention which is representative of the argument advanced by the dialectical theology respecting the relation of the incarnation to the doctrine of Scripture.

First of all, we find in Calvin himself no sense of incongruity between Scripture as being itself the truth of God and Christ as truth incarnate, nor even between an inerrant Scripture and Christ as the focal point of revelation. It is in this same context, in which he insists that Christ is the fountain from which the saints in all ages must have drawn whatever they knew of celestial doctrine, that Calvin delineates for us the process of revelation and particularly the process by which the truth of God became inscripturated. But what is of special interest for us in terms of the present discussion is his estimate of Scripture itself as the inscripturated Word of God. We must not fail to note what Calvin says that "when it pleased God to raise up a more visible form of the church, it was his will that his Word be committed to writing."[10] It is the Word of God that is committed to writing and so

---

[7]*Ibid.*, p. 33.
[8]*Idem.*
[9]*Ibid.*, p. 36.
[10]*Inst.*, IV, viii, 6.

Scripture is the Word inscripturated. So he sums up the case for the whole Old Testament by saying: "That whole body of Scripture, therefore, consisting of the law, the prophets, the psalms, and the histories was the Word of the Lord to the ancient people (*verbum Domini fuit veteri populo*), and to this rule the priests and teachers, to the coming of Christ, were bound to conform their doctrine; nor was it lawful for them to deviate to the right hand or to the left, because their office was wholly confined within these limits, that they would answer the people from the mouth of God."[11] The implication is clear that Scripture, because it is the Word of God written, is the mouth of God and therefore, as we have found repeatedly, is as if we heard the voice of God from heaven.

At this point Calvin does not suppress in the least degree the stupendous import of Christ's advent in the flesh. Christ is the sun of righteousness and, since he has shone upon us, "we have the full splendour of divine truth" and this is "the last and eternal testimony that we shall have" from God.[12] But the significant fact is also that, when Calvin has thus unfolded the splendor, the uniqueness, and finality of the revelation in Christ as the incarnate Son, there is not even the suggestion that Scripture is bereft of any of the finality and authority that belongs to it as the Word or oracle of God written. And not only that there is no retreat; there is the emphatic reaffirmation of this assessment of Scripture. It is just after having asserted that in the Son incarnate God has given "the last and eternal testimony that we shall have from him" that we read: "Let this, therefore, be a fixed axiom that nothing should be admitted in the church as the Word of God (*Dei verbum*) but what is contained first in the law and the prophets and then in the writings of the apostles (*scriptis apostolicis*), and that there is no other method of teaching aright in the church than according to the prescription and norm of this Word."[13] What the apostles did they

---

[11]*Idem.*
[12]*Ibid.*, IV, viii, 7.
[13]*Ibid.*, IV, viii, 8.

did from the Lord and "under the direction and dictation of
the Spirit of Christ."[14] "The apostles," he says, "were the
certain and authentic amanuenses of the Holy Spirit and
therefore their writings are to be received as the oracles of
God."[15]

It should be recognized, therefore, as beyond dispute that
for Calvin there is no incompatibility between Christ as being
himself the incarnate Word of God, the full splendor of divine
truth, the last and eternal testimony of God to us, on the
one hand, and Scripture as the Word of God, invested with
the oracular quality of God's mouth, on the other. And so,
far from there being any necessity to tone down Calvin's
estimate of the nature and effect of inspiration, as set forth
in other places, the case is that, in these very contexts where
the finality and centrality of Christ are most plainly and
eloquently expressed, there also the same concept of inspiration is introduced in order to support the thesis that Scripture is the Word of God written.

But, secondly, not only is it true that in Calvin there is
no sense of incongruity between the finality that belongs to
Christ as the incarnate Word and the finality of Scripture
as the Word of God written, but we may also ask the question: why should we look for any sense of incongruity? Calvin
was a profound thinker and an eminently consistent thinker.
I submit that the reason why these two theses lie side by side
in Calvin without any suggestion of contradiction is precisely
because Calvin was faithful to the testimony of Jesus as God's
last and eternal testimony to us and understood the implications of this same testimony. And I further submit that it
is because Wilhelm Niesel and others like him have failed
to appreciate the implications of the axiom that Jesus is the
focal point of revelation that they institute an antithesis
between Scripture as the veritable Word of God written and
Christ as the incarnate Word.

It is to be confessed without any reserve that Christ as the
Son of God incarnate is the supreme revelation of God. He

---

[14]*Idem.*
[15]*Ibid.*, IV, viii, 9.

is the hypostatic [hypostatic: constituting a distinct personality; distinctly personal (Ed.)] Word, the effulgence of God's glory and the very transcript of his being. When we are confronted with him, we are not only confronted with a revelatory word of God but with God himself manifested in the flesh, and God, be it remembered, in his unabridged identity and majesty. We behold his glory as that of the only-begotten from the Father, full of grace and truth. In him dwells the totality of Godhead bodily. And it must be confessed with Calvin and the whole host of Christian confessors that apart from Christ there is no knowledge unto salvation. Yes, all of this and much more must be said of the transcendent uniqueness and finality of Christ's person and of the revelation that came with him. Here is the incomparable fact of God's revelatory and redemptive accomplishment.

But are we to suppose that all that is involved in this fact, that Jesus Christ is the hypostatic Word, impinges in any way upon the possibility or actuality of an inspired and infallible inscripturated Word? This question lies close to the question that is the most urgent and practical question with which all that has been said of the uniqueness, finality, and centrality of Christ confronts us. For the question is: how do we come into relevant encounter with Jesus as the incarnate Word? It was indeed a great privilege bestowed on those who encountered Jesus in the days of his flesh and heard the gracious words that proceeded from his lips. We have abundant evidence of this sense of privilege on the part of the disciples. But Jesus is not here. And how do *we* come to enjoy this encounter with God manifest in the flesh? It is that question exactly that can be answered only in terms of a Scripture produced by the agency and invested with the property of which Calvin wrote.

It is a fact that Christ as the incarnate Word is never brought into contact with us apart from Scripture. This men like Wilhelm Niesel freely admit. And so there need be no debate on the necessity of the Bible for encounter with the personal Word. But, if so, why should an infallible Scripture in any respect militate against the encounter which, it is admitted, the Bible must minister? In other words, why should the quality of inerrancy prejudice this encounter with the incarnate Lord? Is there some liability inherent in inerrancy as such? To ask these questions is to recognize the fallacy of the premise on which this contention is based. There is nothing belonging to inerrancy as such that is inimical to the interests of encounter with the incarnate and exalted Lord. The obvious fact is that inerrancy is rejected on other grounds, and the argument that encounter with the incarnate Word partakes of a strictly personal character is lugged in to give plausible support to the rejection of biblical infallibility— plausible because it seems to do honor to the centrality and finality of Christ as the incarnate Word when, in reality, the doctrine of biblical inerrancy does not impinge in the least degree upon the glory that belongs to, or the faith exercised in, or the worship rendered to the incarnate Lord.

And not only is it true that there is nothing attaching to biblical inerrancy inconsistent with the uniqueness of the revelation embodied in and given by Christ but it can also be shown how consonant with each other these two tenets are.

The revelation that Christ is and gave to us men cannot be divorced from the witness which he bore to himself in the days of his flesh or from the witness borne to him from the Father in verbal utterance. To think of the revelation Jesus gave apart from the words he spoke and apart from the words spoken from heaven in witness borne to him as the beloved Son of the Father is a pure abstraction. The words Jesus spoke were inspired and infallible. On any other assumption we must abandon the infallibility of Jesus as the incarnate Word as well as the centrality and finality of the revelation he was and bore. This infallibility of his spoken word did not in the least degree interfere with the fact that he was the incarnate Word. Rather, it is correlative with his being the incarnate Word; the former flows necessarily from the latter. The fact that he was *the* truth guaranteed the infallibility of his utterances. The inference is, therefore, patent. Inspired and inerrant words are not in the least inconsistent with the fact that Christ himself is the focal point of revelation but, instead, are indispensable to it. It is the infallible spoken word that certified to the disciples the reality and significance of his own self as the hypostatic Word. Revelatory word was the medium of contact and encounter with him in his identity as the Word incarnate.

We today do not have contact with the Son of God as he was manifested in the days of his flesh; we do not hear him speak as the disciples heard him. But revelatory word is just as indispensable for us as it was for the disciples, if we are to have saving encounter with him as the Word made flesh. Hence there must be some other way by which this indispensable medium of contact is supplied. The only medium is that of Scripture.

It is a striking fact that, however great was the sense of privilege on the part of the disciples who saw and heard and handled and touched the Word of life, these same disciples do not represent those others of us who do not enjoy that privilege as in any way bereft of encounter and fellowship with him in the full reality and benefit of Jesus as the Word made flesh. No, they reiterate in their own way the truth Jesus spoke to Thomas, "Because thou hast seen me, thou hast believed: blessed are they that have not seen, and yet have believed" (John 20:29).

To say the least, it would be strange if believers, who are shut off from the special kind of privilege enjoyed by the disciples and, more particularly, shut off from what was for the disciples the indispensable medium of believing encounter with the incarnate Word, namely, his infallible verbal communication to them, should be placed at the disadvantage of having no infallible verbal revelation. For this would mean a radical difference in respect of a factor which is cardinal in the situation of encounter with the incarnate Word. There is not the slightest hint in the New Testament of this radical differentiation and of the corresponding disadvantage for us.

We must go one step further. There is the clearest evidence that no such disadvantage exists. Our Lord and his apostles appealed to Scripture as a finality. They appealed to it as the Scripture that could not be broken. The evidence supporting this view of Scripture on the part of Christ and the apostles has been repeatedly presented and need not be argued now. This means that an inscripturated Word of God is a mode of verbal revelation that meets the requirements of the type of infallible word which is perfectly suited to the demands of our situation, the situation of which we have been speaking. The witness of our Lord and his apostles is to the effect that no mode of verbal revelation can be more authoritative than that of inscripturation and that no mode of revelation that God has been pleased to furnish to us men is as stable and secure as that of inscripturation.

Hence the sum of the matter is this. Infallible verbal revelation is not inimical to the interests which belong to the centrality and finality of Christ as the incarnate Word. The fact is that infallible words were the indispensable medium of confrontation with him in that capacity. *Inscripturated* verbal revelation is the only mode of such revelation available to us. The quality of infallibility does not in the least degree militate against the purpose to be served by that mode of verbal revelation; it enhances that purpose. The witness of our Lord and his apostles is to a Scripture imbued with that quality. An infallible word revelation does no prejudice to the uniqueness of Christ as the incarnate Word but rather continues to insure for us that which the disciples undoubtedly enjoyed. The absence of any tension in Calvin's thought between what he rightly claimed for Christ as God's ultimate and eternal testimony, on the one hand, and the Scriptures of both Testaments as the Word of God written, on the other, witnesses to his fidelity to the testimony of Jesus himself and to his perception that the Scriptures as God's inscripturated Word, invested with the infallibility of God's own sacred mouth, is correlative with the centrality of Christ as the image of the invisible God and indispensable to the situation in which we are placed in this last era of what is the consummation of the ages.

We come now to the next subdivision of our present study, the relation of Scripture to the internal testimony of the Holy Spirit. We shall deal with this question from the angle of the relation of the internal testimony to the authority of Scripture. This is the direction in which the debate respecting Calvin's position has been turned. It is natural that it should be so; Calvin himself pays a good deal of attention to the question as it is thus oriented.

It is in *Institutes,* I, vii, that Calvin deals specifically with the internal testimony of the Holy Spirit, and the summary at the head of the chapter indicates the extent to which this subject is related to the question of the authority of Scripture. "By what testimony ought the Scripture to be established, namely, of the Spirit: in order that its authority may remain certain; and that it is a wicked invention to say that the faith of Scripture depends upon the judgment of the church." And the first sentence in this chapter indicates the same. "Before I proceed any further, it is proper to introduce some observations on the authority of Scripture, not only to prepare our minds to receive it with reverence but also to remove every doubt."[16]

When we speak of the authority of Scripture, we must distinguish between the authority that is intrinsic to Scripture and our persuasion or conviction that it is authoritative. This is the distinction between that which *imparts* authority to Scripture and that which is the *source* of our conviction that it is authoritative, between that in which the authority resides and that from which our assurance proceeds. It is the distinction between objectivity and subjectivity as it pertains to this question.

It may have to be conceded that this distinction is not as clearly formulated in Calvin as we might desire. At least, as far as the term "authority" is concerned, there appears to be some ambiguity. In the 1539 edition of the *Institutes*[17] he says that the authority of Scripture is to be sought from the internal testimony of the Holy Spirit. And there are statements in the definitive edition which are similar. If Calvin means that the authority of Scripture rests upon or is derived from the internal testimony, then it does not rest upon that

---

[16]*Ibid.,* I, vii, 1.
[17]In this edition *cf.* I, 24.

which is intrinsic to Scripture by reason of the activity by which it was produced. On the other hand, there is so much evidence in Calvin to the effect that the authority resides in the divine speaker and, therefore, in that which Scripture inherently is that, in respect of *authority*, we are pointed in a different direction.

Hence we should not be surprised that some of Calvin's interpreters allege that he bases the authority of Scripture to some extent upon the internal testimony. When R. Seeberg says that Calvin grounds the authority of the Scriptures partly upon their divine dictation and partly upon the testimony of the Holy Spirit,[18] we must understand how easily this interpretation could be inferred from Calvin's own remarks. E. A. Dowey, notwithstanding the excellence of his treatment of Calvin's doctrine of Scripture, can write as follows: "True enough, the Bible has intrinsic validity. But this does not constitute its authority or even one source of its authority. The authority derives solely from the inner witness of God himself through which the intrinsic validity or inherent truth of the sacred oracles is recognized and confirmed."[19] And Dowey adds that the internal testimony of the Holy Spirit "is meant to take the weight of the authority of Scripture off of unstable supports and rest it solely upon the 'author,' God."[20] It is to be admitted that these statements of Dowey scarcely cohere with other statements which reflect a more accurate perception of the distinction between intrinsic authority and the accreditation of that authority, between the authority as such and authority with us.[21]

If, as Seeberg maintains, Calvin grounds the authority of Scripture upon the inspiration of Scripture and the internal testimony of the Spirit, the most reasonable view would be that the term "authority" is not used in precisely the same sense in both cases; that when authority is grounded in divine

---

[18]Reinhold Seeberg: *Lehrbuch der Dogmengeschichte,* IV, 2, Erlangen, 1920, p. 569; *cf.* E.T. by Charles E. Hay, Philadelphia, 1905, II, pp. 395f.
[19]*Op. cit.,* p. 108.
[20]*Ibid.,* p. 109.
[21]*Cf. ibid.,* p. 111.

authorship Calvin is thinking of the authority intrinsic to
Scripture and therefore objective to us, whereas, when authority is conceived of as established by the internal testimony,
he is thinking of the authority as registered or, for that matter,
established in our minds. It is quite apparent that these two
senses should not be confused. And if this inference as to
Calvin's twofold use of the term "authority" is correct, it
would be altogether incorrect and confusing to say that
authority in the first sense is grounded in the internal testimony, just as it would be equally confusing to say that
authority in the second sense is derived from inspiration. If
Calvin at any time grounds the authority of Scripture in the
internal testimony, our only conclusion must be that he must
be thinking in such a case of authority *with us,* that is, of
authority as registered in our hearts, and not at all of the
authority intrinsic to Scripture by reason of its inspiration.
We are driven to this conclusion by a series of considerations
derived particularly from the chapters in the *Institutes,* directly
devoted to the question.

1. It is instructive to observe the precise connections in
which the term "authority" occurs in Calvin's exposition of
this topic. With reference to the Scriptures as the only extant
oracles of God he says that "they obtain complete authority
with believers only when they are persuaded that they proceeded from heaven."[22] Now it is plain that here Calvin is
dealing with the *persuasion* which he proceeds to show is
derived from the internal testimony. But he is not in the
least suggesting that the authority itself is derived from this
source. It is the "authority with believers" (*apud fideles
autoritatem*). In other words, he is dealing with the authority as registered in the hearts of believers. Furthermore, this
authority is obtained when they are assured that the Scriptures proceeded from heaven. It is, therefore, the *recognition*
of heavenly origin that induces the conviction. But it is
the heavenly origin itself that invests the Scripture with the
authority recognized. Again we read: "It must be maintained,

---

[22]*Inst.,* I, vii, 1.

as I have already asserted, that the faith of this doctrine is not established until we are indubitably persuaded that God is its author. Hence the highest proof of Scripture is always taken from the character of God the speaker."[23] That "God is its author" is that of which we are persuaded. Divine authorship is the antecedent fact and is not created by our persuasion nor by that which induces this recognition on our part. It is divine authorship, therefore, that invests Scripture with authority and it is not by the internal testimony that this authorship is effected.

In another place Calvin says: "Without this certainty, better and stronger than any human judgment, in vain will the authority of Scripture be defended by arguments, or established by the consent of the church, or confirmed by other supports."[24] The certainty referred to is that produced by the internal testimony of the Spirit. But the authority is the authority of the Scripture, that which belongs to it as Scripture by divine inspiration, and not that which is created by the internal testimony. It is that which may be made the subject of demonstration and argument because the Scripture exhibits the plainest evidence that it is God who speaks in it. It is not, however, the internal testimony that invests Scripture with that quality but the agency of the Spirit by which it was produced. And Calvin's point here is simply that assured faith in Scripture will never be induced by argument but proceeds only from the work of the Spirit in our hearts. So in this passage again the *authority* is something quite distinct from the internal testimony and is conceived of as that which exists antecedently to the effectual work of the Spirit in us.

2. When Calvin deals with the internal testimony of the Holy Spirit, it is always related in one way or another to our persuasion and to the agency by which this *persuasion* is secured. In other words, the internal testimony has efficiency and relevance in respect of assurance in our minds. Let us listen to a catena of quotations. The question in his own

---

[23]*Ibid.*, I, vii, 4.
[24]*Ibid.*, I, viii, 1.

words is: "Who will assure us that they [the Scriptures] came
forth from God?"[25] "If we wish to consult most effectually
with our consciences...this persuasion must be sought from
the secret testimony of the Spirit." "Though any one vindicates
the sacred word of God from the aspersions of men, yet it will
not fix in the heart the certitude which is necessary to piety."
"For as God alone is a sufficient witness to himself in his own
word, so also the word will never gain credit in the hearts
of men until it is sealed by the internal testimony of the Spirit.
It is necessary, therefore, that the same Spirit who spoke by
the mouth of the prophets penetrate into our hearts in order
that he might persuade us that they faithfully delivered what
had been divinely entrusted to them." "The Spirit," he
continues, "is denominated a seal and an earnest for the
confirmation of the faith of the godly, because, until he
illuminates their minds, they always fluctuate amidst a multi-
tude of doubts."[26] "Let it remain then a fixed truth that those
whom the Spirit inwardly teaches firmly acquiesce in the
Scripture, and that the same is self-authenticating (*autopiston*)
and that it ought not to be made the subject of demonstration
and arguments but obtains the certitude which it deserves
with us from the testimony of the Spirit. For although it
conciliates our reverence by its own majesty, nevertheless it
seriously affects us only when it is sealed on our hearts by the
Spirit. Therefore being illuminated by his virtue we now
believe that the Scripture is from God, not by our own judgment or that of others, but, in a way that transcends human
judgment, we are indubitably convinced (*certo certius consti-
tuimus*)...that it has flowed to us from the very mouth of
God by the ministry of men.... Only let it be known that
that alone is true faith which the Spirit of God seals in our
hearts."[27] Finally, in his comments on I John 2:27, he says:
"The Spirit is like a seal, by which the truth of God is testified
to us. When he adds, 'and is no lie,' by this particular he
designates another office of the Spirit, namely, that he endues

---

[25]*Ibid.*, I, vii, 1.
[26]*Ibid.*, I, vii, 4.
[27]*Ibid.*, I, vii, 5.

us with judgment and discernment, lest we should be deceived by a lie, lest we should hesitate or be perplexed, lest we should vacillate in doubtful things."[28] It should, therefore, be clear that the function of the internal testimony is, after all, what the term "internal" implies, namely, an operation in our minds directed to the persuasion, assurance, conviction appropriate to that which Scripture intrinsically is.

3. There is the sustained insistence on Calvin's part upon the intrinsic character of Scripture and of the evidence which Scripture contains of its intrinsic divinity. "The Scripture exhibits as clear evidence of its truth as white and black things do of their colour, or sweet and bitter things of their taste."[29] "It is true that, if we were to argue the point, many things might be adduced which easily prove that, if there is a God in heaven, the law, and the prophecies, and the gospel have proceeded from him.... The Scripture exhibits the clearest evidences of God speaking in it, which manifests its doctrine to be divine.... If we bring to it pure eyes and sound minds, the majesty of God will immediately confront us, which will subdue our presumption and compel us to obedience."[30] And when Calvin speaks of "the majesty of the Spirit," he is not referring to the internal testimony but to the quality belonging to Scripture by reason of divine inspiration. Referring to the prophets, he says, that, wherever we read, "that majesty of the Spirit, of which I have spoken, is everywhere conspicuous."[31] "The same thing is true of Paul and Peter in whose writings, although most are blind to it, that same heavenly majesty attracts and rivets the attention of all."[32] "There are other reasons neither few nor invalid by which the Scripture's own dignity and majesty are not only maintained in the minds of the godly but also completely vindicated against the cavils of slanderers."[33]

---

[28]*Comm. ad* I John 2:27.
[29]*Inst.*, I, vii, 2.
[30]*Ibid.*, I, vii, 4.
[31]*Ibid.*, I, viii, 2.
[32]*Ibid.*, I, viii, 11.
[33]*Ibid.*, I, viii, 13.

The sum of this is clear. God speaks in Scripture. In it he opens his sacred mouth. In Scripture the majesty of God confronts us. This divinity inheres in the Scripture and it therefore exhibits the plainest evidence that it is God's Word. When we bring sound minds it compels our submission and obedience. And our conclusion must be that this is but another way of saying that Scripture is by its nature divinely authoritative. These quotations also illumine for us what Calvin means when he says that Scripture is "self-authenticating." The predicate itself should advise us that he is not referring here to the internal testimony. For of *Scripture* he says "it is self-authenticating" (*autopistos*). He must be referring to that evidence which the Scripture inherently contains of its divine origin, character, and authority, the evidence which demonstrates that it is God himself who speaks in it. It is only those who are inwardly taught by the Spirit who perceive this evidence and only from them does it receive the credit it deserves. But it should be equally clear that the evidence by which Scripture authenticates itself is the evidence it contains and not the internal testimony.

4. There is a fourth consideration that supports this same conclusion. It is that Calvin speaks of the internal testimony as confirmation and seal. "For as God alone is a sufficient witness to himself in his own word, so also the word will never gain credit in the hearts of men until it is sealed by the internal testimony of the Spirit."[34] "For although it conciliates our reverence by its own majesty, then only does it seriously affect us when it is sealed on our hearts by the Spirit."[35] "Only let it be known that that alone is true faith which the Spirit seals on our hearts."[36] "The office of the Spirit, therefore, who is promised to us...is to seal to our hearts that same doctrine which is commended to us through the gospel."[37] It should be apparent that the function of a seal is simply to confirm and authenticate what is intrinsically and

---

[34]*Ibid.*, I, vii, 4.
[35]*Ibid.*, I, vii, 5.
[36]*Idem.*
[37]*Ibid.*, I, ix, 1.

antecedently true. The seal adds nothing by way of content. If it is by the Spirit that the authority is sealed, the authority is presupposed and is no more created by the seal than is the truth of a promise created by its confirmation. So the simple notion of seal is, of itself, evidence that in Calvin's conception the internal testimony does not impart authority to Scripture but merely confirms to us the authority which is antecedent and extrinsic to the internal testimony itself.

Suffice it to conclude by appeal to one passage which, if any doubt should still persist, places beyond all question the thesis that for Calvin the authority of Scripture does not reside in the internal testimony but in that which Scripture is by reason of divine inspiration. It is that passage dealt with already which, as much as, if not more than, any other statement in the whole range of his works enunciates his concept of Scripture as to its origin, character, and authority, namely his comments on II Timothy 3:16. We read: "First he [Paul] commends the Scripture from its authority, and then on account of the utility that springs therefrom. In order that he may uphold the authority of Scripture he declares that it is divinely inspired. For if it be so it is beyond all controversy that men ought to receive it with reverence." Two facts are incontestable. (1) Here Calvin says nothing of the internal testimony. He deals with that in the succeeding paragraph where he speaks of it as the witness which is borne to our hearts. (2) It is divine inspiration that is the authority-imparting factor and that for which it ought to be received with reverence. And so there is no room for question that it is to the fact of inspiration that Calvin would appeal in support of the proposition that Scripture is authoritative. And this is but to confirm what we have found repeatedly that the authority *resides* in its authorship and not in that by which divine authorship is confirmed.

Chapter III

Calvin on the Sovereignty of God

Chapter III

Calvin on the Sovereignty of God

No treatment of the subject of God's sovereignty has surpassed in depth of thought, in reverence of approach, and in eloquence of expression that which we find in the last three chapters of Book I of the *Institutes*. It is sufficient to be reminded of one or two of the classic statements which we find in these chapters to appreciate anew the intensity of Calvin's faith in the all-pervasive and over-ruling providence of God. "So it must be concluded," he says, "that while the turbulent state of the world deprives us of judgment, God, by the pure light of his own righteousness and wisdom, regulates these very commotions in the most exact order and directs them to their proper end."[1] Or, again, it is Calvin who has given us the formula which has become in many Reformed circles a household word for thankfulness, resignation, and hope. The necessary consequences of the knowledge that God governs all creatures, including the devil himself, for the benefit and safety of his people, are "gratitude in prosperity, patience in adversity, and a wonderful security respecting the future."[2]

What then for Calvin does the sovereignty of God mean? I suppose that no Christian in the catholic tradition, not to speak of the evangelical and Reformed traditions, will formally deny the sovereignty of God. For to say that God is sovereign is but to affirm that God is one and that God is God. But we may not be misled by the formal use of vocables. It

---

[1] *Inst.*, I, xvii, 1.
[2] *Ibid.*, I, xvii, 7.

is possible for us to profess the sovereignty of God and deny
it in the particulars in which this sovereignty is expressed,
to assert a universal but evade the particularities. It is precisely in this respect that Calvin's doctrine of the sovereignty
of God is to be assessed and appreciated.

The Sovereignty of God in Decree

That Calvin regards everything that occurs as embraced
in the eternal decree of God lies on the face of his teaching
at every point where he finds occasion to reflect on this subject.
While repudiating the Stoic doctrine of necessity, arising from
a perpetual intertwining and confused series of causes contained in nature, he is insistent that God is the arbiter and
governor of all things "who, of his own wisdom, from the
remotest eternity, decreed what he would do, and now by
his own power executes what he has decreed. Whence we
assert, that, not only the heaven and the earth and inanimate
creatures, but also the deliberations and volitions of men are
so governed by his providence that they are directed exactly
to their destined end"[3] and thus nothing happens fortuitously
or contingently. "The will of God is the supreme and first
cause of all things, because nothing happens but by his command or permission."[4] And in his extensive tract on *The
Eternal Predestination of God,* dedicated on January 1, 1552,
he says to the same effect that "the hand of God no less rules
the internal affections than it precedes the external acts, and
that God does not perform by the hand of men those things
which he has decreed without first working in their hearts the
very will which precedes their acts."[5]

It is of greater relevance to us in the theological situation
in which we are placed today to understand and assess the
position which Calvin espoused and defended on the question -

---

[3] *Ibid.,* I, xvi, 8.
[4] *Idem.,* John Allen's translation.
[5] *De Aeterna Dei Praedestinatione,* in *Opera* (Brunswick, 1870), VIII, col.
358; *cf.* E.T. by Henry Cole: *Calvin's Calvinism,* London, 1927, p. 243.
It is regrettable that Cole unnecessarily embellishes his translation. I have
often given my own renderings.

which brings to focal and acute expression his doctrine of the eternal decree. It is that concerned with the question of election and reprobation. It is of interest that in his earliest commentary, that on the Epistle to the Romans, dedicated at Strassburg on October 18, 1539, he provides us with his thought on this question at a comparatively early age. It is well for us to take heed to Calvin's own advice that "the predestination of God is indeed a labyrinth from which the mind of man can by no means extricate itself." But we are not for that reason to avoid every thought of it. For "the Holy Spirit," he says, "has taught us nothing but what it behooves us to know.... Let this then be our sacred rule, to seek to know nothing concerning it, except what Scripture teaches us; when the Lord closes his holy mouth, let us also stop the way, that we may go no further."[6]

While Calvin thus properly cautions us to be silent when God closes his own sacred mouth and to seek to know nothing but what God teaches us in Scripture, he at the same time upbraids that false modesty that suppresses the doctrine of Scripture and pleads caution as an excuse to refrain from subscribing to its witness. This kind of caution he brands as preposterous; the honor of God is not to be protected by the pretended modesty which refuses to listen to what God has revealed. When God has spoken we cannot remain ignorant without loss and harm.[7] What Calvin is maintaining in these contexts is the free and absolute sovereignty of God in the discrimination that exists among men in respect of election, on the one hand, and reprobation, on the other. In the matter of election he insists that "the salvation of believers depends on the eternal election of God, for which no cause or reason can be rendered but his own gratuitous good pleasure."[8] "Inasmuch as God elects some and reprobates others, the cause is not to be found in anything else but in his own purpose."[9] It would be unnecessary and

---

[6]*Comm. ad* Rom. 9:14; *cf.* E.T. by John Owen.
[7]*Cf. De Aeterna Dei Praedestinatione,* as cited, coll. 263f.; E.T., pp. 34f.
[8]*Ibid.,* col. 270; E.T., p. 44.
[9]*Comm. ad* Rom. 9:14.

unduly burdensome at this time to show how Calvin rejects
the subterfuge of appeal to foreknowledge in order to evade
the force of the emphasis which Scripture places upon the
pure sovereignty of God's election of some and rejection of
others. Suffice it to quote one word of his in this connection.
"The foreknowledge of God, which Paul mentions, is not a
bare prescience, as some unwise persons absurdly imagine,
but the adoption by which he had always distinguished his
children from the reprobate."[10]

In connection with election Calvin fully recognizes that this
election was in Christ. Nothing, however, could be more
remote from Calvin's thought than to suppose that this fact
in the least interferes with the pure sovereignty and particu-
larism of the election itself. On the contrary, he says expressly
that this is the confirmation that "the election is free; for
if we were chosen *in* Christ, it is not of ourselves."[11] And
the practical import for us of this truth is that no one should
seek confidence in his own election anywhere else than in
Christ. "Christ, therefore, is both the clear glass in which
we are called upon to behold the eternal and hidden election
of God, and also the earnest and pledge."[12] Referring to John
17:6, he says, "We see here that God begins with himself
(a se ipso), when he condescends to elect us: but he will have
us to begin with Christ in order that we may know that we are
reckoned among that peculiar people."[13] "Election, indeed,
is prior to faith, but it is learned by faith."[14]

As respects reprobation we are required to ask, in the main,
two questions. The first question concerns what has been
called its ultimacy. In the esteem of Calvin, is the passing
over or rejection of the non-elect as eternal and as sovereign,
in that sense as ultimate, as the choosing of the elect to eternal
salvation? It appears to me that the frequency and the clarity
with which Calvin deals with this question leave no doubt

---

[10]*Comm. ad* Rom. 8:29; E.T. by John Owen.
[11]*Comm. ad* Eph. 1:4.
[12]*De Aeterna Dei Praedestinatione,* as cited, col. 318; *cf.* E.T., p. 132.
[13]*Ibid.,* col. 319; *cf.* E.T., p. 133.
[14]*Ibid.,* col. 318; *cf.* E.T., p. 133.

that the answer must be affirmative. It needs to be appreciated that his long dissertation on *The Eternal Predestination of God* was directed chiefly against the thesis of Pighius that the origin of reprobation was God's foreknowledge that some would remain to the last in contempt of divine grace and so the wicked deprive themselves of the benefit of universal election. Pighius denied that certain persons were absolutely appointed to destruction.[15] It is on this background that we must understand Calvin's repeated assertions to the contrary. He appeals to Augustine who, "tracing the beginning of election to the gratuitous will of God, places reprobation in his mere will likewise."[16] "There is," he continues, "most certainly an inseparable connection between the elect and the reprobate, so that the election, of which the apostle speaks, cannot consist unless we confess that God separated from others certain persons whom it pleased him thus to separate."[17] "It is indeed true that the reprobate bring upon themselves the wrath of God by their own depravity, and that they daily hasten on to the falling of its weight upon their own heads. But it must be confessed that the apostle is here treating of that difference which proceeds from the secret judgment of God."[18]

In his commentary on Romans 9 Calvin likewise says: "That our mind may be satisfied with the difference which exists between the elect and the reprobate, and may not inquire for any cause higher than the divine will, his [Paul's] purpose was to convince us of this — that it seems good to God to illuminate some that they may be saved, and to blind others that they may perish: for we ought particularly to notice these words, *to* whom he wills, and, *whom he wills*: beyond this he allows us not to proceed."[19] "It is indeed evident that no cause is adduced higher than the will of God. Since there was a ready answer, that the difference depends on

---

[15]*Cf. Ibid.,* coll. 259f.; E.T., pp. 27f.
[16]*Ibid.,* col. 267; *cf.* E.T., p. 41.
[17]*Ibid.,* col. 270; *cf.* E.T., p. 45.
[18]*Ibid.,* col. 288; *cf.* E.T., pp. 76f.
[19]*Comm. ad* Rom. 9:18; E.T. by John Owen.

just reasons, why did not Paul adopt such a brief reply? But he placed the will of God in the highest rank for this reason, — that it alone may suffice us for all other causes. No doubt, if the objection had been false... a refutation would not have been rejected by Paul. The ungodly object and say, that men are exempted from blame, if the will of God holds the first place in their salvation, or in their perdition. Does Paul deny this? Nay, by his answer he confirms it, that God determines concerning men, as it seems good to him...for he assigns, by his own right, whatever lot he pleases to what he forms."[20]

These quotations are sufficient to show that no doubt can be entertained respecting Calvin's position that the differentiation that exists among men finds its explanation in the sovereign discrimination which God in his eternal counsel was pleased to make and that the passing by and rejection of the reprobate, in respect of differentiation and the diverse destiny entailed, are correlative with the election of those appointed to salvation. The sovereign will of God as the highest and ultimate cause is just as rigorously posited in reprobation as it is in election. And if the formula, "the equal ultimacy of election and reprobation" is intended to denote this precise consideration, then there can be no room for hesitation in asserting that Calvin would have subscribed to that formula.

On the other hand, in respect of ultimacy, if the question is that of consequent destiny, there likewise needs to be no doubt but that for Calvin ultimate and irreversible perdition is coextensive with the decree of reprobation. It is scarcely necessary to adduce evidence in support of this conclusion. The way in which Calvin discusses the whole question of reprobation would be nullified as to its relevance and necessity if reprobation did not have as its implication eternal destruction, or election eternal salvation. But one or two quotations may be offered to confirm this conclusion. "As the blessing of the covenant separates the Israelitic nation from all other people, so the election of God makes a distinction

---

[20]*Comm. ad* Rom. 9:20; E.T. by John Owen.

between men in that nation, while he predestinates some to salvation, and others to eternal condemnation."[21] "Paul teaches us, that the ruin of the wicked is not only foreseen by the Lord, but also ordained by his counsel and his will; and Solomon teaches us the same thing, — that not only the destruction of the wicked is foreknown, but that the wicked themselves have been created for this very end — that they may perish (Prov. 16:4)."[22]

The second question that arises in connection with reprobation is one that must never be overlooked. If we do not take account of this consideration we fail to appreciate the radical distinction that obtains between the predestination to life, which belongs to election, and the foreordination to death, which inheres in reprobation. Calvin insisted, as we have found, and insisted rightly, that in the differentiation between election and reprobation we must seek for no higher or more ultimate cause than the sovereign will of God and that the pure sovereignty of God's good pleasure is the origin and explanation of reprobation no less than of election. But there is a factor in reprobation that does not enter into the salvation which is the fruit of election. This factor is that reprobation cannot be conceived of apart from the everlasting condemnation which it involves and condemnation always presupposes guilt and ill-desert. Guilt and ill-desert attach themselves to us. And, therefore, reprobation must never be conceived of apart from the ground or basis which resides in us for the condemnation that reprobation entails. In a word, the ground of condemnation is sin and sin alone. And sin is ours and ours alone. So reprobation always finds in men themselves a basis which never can be applied to the salvation which is the issue of election. To reiterate, the ground of the discrimination that exists among men is, as Calvin has maintained, the sovereign will of God and that alone. But the ground of the damnation to which the reprobate are consigned is sin and sin alone.

---

[21]*Comm. ad* Rom. 9:11; E.T. by John Owen.
[22]*Comm. ad* Rom. 9:18; E.T. by John Owen.

Calvin has not failed to recognize this distinction. We have an intimation of this in his statement: "In the salvation of the godly nothing higher must be sought than the goodness of God, and nothing higher in the perdition of the reprobate than his just severity."[23] It is that term "just severity" (*justa severitas*) that points to the exercise of judicial infliction in the matter of reprobation, that is, the execution of just judgment. It indicates that the judical enters into the concept of reprobation. And he does not permit us to be in any doubt as to what he means by "just severity." He has his own way of enunciating this truth, and the import is clear. "It is indeed true," he says, "that here is the proximate cause of reprobation, because we are all cursed in Adam."[24] And when he inveighs against the clamor of the ungodly he says: "being not content with defending themselves, they make God guilty instead of themselves; and then, after having devolved upon him the blame of their own condemnation, they become indignant against his great power."[25] Again he says that although the secret predestination of God is the first cause and "superior to all other causes, *so* the corruption and wickedness of the ungodly afford a reason and an occasion for the judgments of God" (*locum materiamque praebet Dei judiciis*).[26] "The ungodly are indeed, on account of their evil deeds, visited by God's judgment with blindness; but if we seek for the source (*fontem*) of their ruin, we must come to this, that being accursed by God, they cannot by all their deeds, sayings, and purposes, get and obtain anything but a curse."[27]

So it is quite apparent that Calvin does not think of reprobation as taking effect apart from the curse that rests upon sin. Sin is the proximate cause of damnation, and no man can justly plead that punishment executed is the consequence

---

[23]*Comm. ad* Rom. 9:11; E.T. by John Owen.
[24]*Idem.*
[25]*Comm. ad* Rom. 9:19; E.T. by John Owen.
[26]*Comm. ad* Rom. 9:30.
[27]*Comm. ad* Rom. 11:7.

of aught but that for which he is to be blamed. It is therefore "just severity."

So Calvin is fully cognizant of the judicial aspect of reprobation. We should not be doing justice to Calvin, however, were we to overlook the contexts in which these references to sin as "the proximate cause of reprobation" occur. The term "proximate cause," of itself, advises us that there is a more ultimate cause and this is stated in the same sentence to be "the bare and simple good pleasure of God" in electing and reprobating by his own will. When he speaks of "the blame of their own damnation," which men seek to load upon God, it is in a context in which the accent falls upon the fact that "those who perish have been destined by the will of God to destruction" and that the will of God holds the first place in salvation and perdition. And when he admits that the pravity and wickedness of the ungodly provide the material for God's judgments, yet he protests that it is to invert all order to set up causes "above the secret predestination of God."[28] What may we infer as to the reason for this jealousy with respect to the sovereign will and good pleasure of God? There can be but one answer.

When Calvin establishes the judicial factor in reprobation, he is bound to reckon with the fact that the *reason* why some are consigned to the curse, which we all inherit from Adam, and others are predestined to salvation is simply and solely the sovereign will of God. After all, ill-desert is not the reason for the discrimination, though it is the ground for the condemnation executed. And it is the note of secret predestination that is uppermost in Calvin's thought at these points, because this is the only explanation why the reprobate are left to reap the curse which their evil deeds deserve and for which they have no answer before God. This is why we are compelled to take account of the ultimacy, even in the matter of the judicial or penal aspect of reprobation, of the sovereignty of God's will, a sovereignty which is not one whit less sover-

---

[28]*Comm. ad* Rom. 9:30.

eignly differentiating at the point of reprobation than it is
at the point of election to life.

The formula, "the equal ultimacy of election and reprobation" is not one that, in my judgment, is most felicitous
because it is liable, by reason of its brevity, to obscure the
penal, judicial, and hell-deserving ingredient which must enter
into the concept of reprobation. But we must not affirm less
than the equal ultimacy of the pure sovereignty of God's good
pleasure in election and reprobation and that the sovereign
discrimination that is exemplified in election is brought to
bear upon reprobation at the point of its judicial execution
as well as at the point of preterition. This I believe is the
precipitate of Calvin's thinking on this topic, and I am not
able to regard it as other than the precipitate of biblical teaching.

We should not, however, be giving a fair transcript of Calvin's teaching on this subject if we omitted to make mention
of his warning. "Proud men clamour, because Paul, admitting
that men are rejected or chosen by the secret counsel of God,
alleges no cause; as though the Spirit of God were silent for
want of reason, and not rather, that by his silence he reminds
us, that a mystery which our minds cannot comprehend ought
to be reverently adored, and that he thus checks the wanton-
ness of human curiosity. Let us then know, that God does
for no other reason refrain from speaking, but that he sees
that we cannot contain his immense wisdom in our small
measure; and thus regarding our weakness, he leads us to
moderation and sobriety."[29] "And far be it from any one
of the faithful to be ashamed to confess his ignorance of that
which the Lord God has enveloped in the blaze of his own
inaccessible light."[30]

The Sovereignty of God in His Providence

The providence of God embraces all events, past, present,
and future, and applies to the evil as much as to the good,

---

[29]*Comm. ad* Rom. 9:20; E.T. by John Owen.
[30]*De Aeterna Dei Praedestinatione*, as cited, col. 316; E.T., p. 128.

to sinful acts as much as to the holy acts of men and angels. Unsanctified sense is liable to conceive of providence as consisting simply in the unfolding of potencies and virtues implanted in the world at its creation and so the utmost of its adoration is to perceive the wisdom, power, and goodness of God in the work of creation. It conceives of God as a mere spectator. For the believer the presence of God appears no less in the perpetual government of the world than in its origin. Perhaps the most distinctive emphasis in this connection is Calvin's insistence that providence does not consist in a general motion or superintendence but that all events whatsoever are governed by the secret counsel and directed by the present hand of God (*occulto Dei consilio gubernari ... praesenti Dei manu diriguntur*). Calvin does not deny but rather asserts that created things are endowed with properties and laws which operate according to their nature. Yet they are only instruments into which God infuses as much efficacy as he wills and according to his own will turns to this or that action. The sun, for example, "the godly man does not regard as the principal or necessary cause of those things which existed before the creation of the sun but only an instrument which God uses, because he so wills, since he could dispense with it and act directly without any more difficulty."[31] God made the sun to stand still (Josh. 10:13) to testify that "the sun does not daily rise and set by a secret instinct of nature but that he himself governs its course to renew the memory of his fatherly favour towards us."[32] God's omnipotence is not a vain, idle, and, as it were, slumbering potency but a vigilant, efficacious, and operative agency constantly exerted on every distinct and particular movement (*ad singulas et particulares motus*). Not a drop of rain falls and no wind ever blows but at the special command of God (*speciali Dei jussu*).[33] Every year, month, and day is governed by a new and special providence of God (*nova et speciali*

---

[31]*Inst.*, I, xvi, 2.
[32]*Idem*.
[33]*Ibid.*, I, xvi, 7.

Dei providentia temperari).[34] Chance and fortune do not belong to a Christian man's vocabulary. Events are often fortuitous to us because their order, reason, end, and necessity are hid in the counsel of God and are not apprehended by the mind of man. But they are not fortuitous for God—they proceed from his will.

This insistence upon the ever-present and ever-active will of God in each particular movement obviously rules out the notion of bare permission. But Calvin takes pains to reflect on this subterfuge. It is particularly in connection with the sinful acts of Satan and of wicked men that the postulate of bare permission appears to offer escape from the allegation that the presence of the will and agency of God would be inconsistent with the responsibility and guilt which devolve upon the perpetrators of iniquity. In Calvin's esteem, this resort to the idea of permission is only to evade the difficulty. For "that men can effect nothing but by the secret will of God nor can they be exercised in deliberating anything but what he has previously with himself decreed and determines by his secret direction is proved by innumerable and express testimonies."[35] "Whatever is attempted by men, or by Satan himself, God still holds the helm in order to turn all their attempts to the execution of his judgments."[35] So it is nugatory and insipid to substitute for the providence of God a bare permission. The very "conceptions we form in our minds are directed by the secret inspiration of God to the end which he has designed" (*arcana Dei inspiratione ad suum finem dirigi*).[36]

It is obvious what questions arise in connection with this doctrine. And Calvin was well aware of the objections and faced up squarely to their apparent validity. There is, first of all, the question of authorship. Is not God, therefore, the author of the crimes which the instruments of iniquity conceive and perpetrate? At certain points Calvin does speak of God as author and cause. According to Scripture God

[34]*Idem.*
[35]*Ibid.*, I, xviii, 1.
[36]*Ibid.*, I, xviii, 2.

"himself is said to give men over to a reprobate mind and cast them into vile lusts, because he is the principal author (*praecipuus autor*) of his own righteous vengeance, and Satan is only the minister of it."[37] Again he says: "And I have already sufficiently shown that God is called the author (*autor*) of all these things which these censors wish to happen merely by his idle permission."[38]

There are, however, certain qualifications which must be appreciated if we are to assess these statements correctly. Calvin is equally emphatic to the effect that God is not the *author* of sin. With respect to Adam's fall he says expressly, that although God ordained the fall of Adam, "I so assert it as by no means to concede that God was the author."[39] "But *how* it was that God, by his foreknowledge and decree, ordained what should take place respecting man, and yet so ordained it without his being himself in the least a participator of the fault, or being at all the author (*autor*) or the approver of the transgression; *how* this was, I repeat, is a secret manifestly far too deep to be penetrated by the human mind, nor am I ashamed to confess our ignorance. And far be it from any of the faithful to be ashamed to confess his ignorance of that which the Lord envelops in the blaze of his own inaccessible light."[40]

Furthermore, Calvin will allow for no equivocation on the principle that in those operations which are common to God and men God is free from all fault and contracts no defilement from men's vices. No one has expended more care than Calvin in developing the distinction in respect of the motive, reason, and end by which men are actuated in the commission of sin and the motive, reason, and end by which God makes the vices of men to fulfil his holy purposes. "So great is the difference," he says in quoting from Augustine, "between what belongs to the human will, and what to the divine, and between the ends to which the will of every one is to be referred, for appro-

---

[37]*Idem.*
[38]*Ibid.*, I, xviii, 3.
[39]*De Aeterna Dei Praedestinatione*, as cited, col. 315; *cf.* E.T., p. 126.
[40]*Ibid.*, col. 316; *cf.* E.T., p. 128.

bation or censure. For God fulfils his righteous will by the
wicked wills of wicked men."[41] There is a complete disparity
between the wills of wicked men and the will of God which
is operative in the same event. When men sin they do not
perform evil actions with the motive or design of promoting
the will of God but because they are inflamed with the violence
of their own passions and deliberately strive to oppose him.
"God only requires of us conformity to his precepts. If we
do anything contrary to them, it is not obedience, but con-
tumacy and transgression... they [men] can lay no blame
upon God, for they find in themselves nothing but evil, and
in him only a legitimate use of their wickedness."[42] There
is thus a coincidence of the wicked wills of wicked men and
the holy will of God. Both are operative in and converge
upon the same event, and yet God contracts no defilement
from the perversity which is the instrument of his holy designs.
The difficulty this may pose for our understanding arises from
the fact that "because of the weakness of our mind we do
not comprehend how in different respects (*diverso modo*) he
does not will and wills the same thing" (*nolit fieri et velit*).[43]

It is not only, however, the disparity that exists between the
wicked wills of men and the holy will of God, as both converge upon the same event, but also the disparity that exists
within the will of God. There is a twofold aspect to the will
of God. And there is the *disparity* between the decretive will
and the preceptive will, between the determinations of his
secret counsel that certain events will come to pass and the
prescriptions of his revealed will to us that we do not bring
these events to pass. It cannot be gainsaid that God decretively
wills what he preceptively forbids and decretively forbids what
he preceptively commands. It is precisely in this consideration
that the doctrine of God's sovereignty is focused most acutely
with its demands for our faith and reverence. If I am not
mistaken it is at this point that the sovereignty of God makes
the human mind reel as it does nowhere else in connection

---

[41]*Inst.*, I, xviii, 3.
[42]*Ibid.*, I, xvii, 5; E.T. by John Allen.
[43]*Ibid.*, I, xviii, 3.

with this topic. It should be so. It is the sanctified understanding that reels. And it is not the mark of intelligence to allege or claim a ready resolution of the apparent contradiction with which it confronts us. How can God say: this comes to pass by my infallible foreordination and providence, and also say to us: this thou shalt not bring to pass?

Calvin was well aware of this question and he did not tone down the mystery with which it confronts us. He is constantly refuting, by appeal to Scripture, the objections which unbelief registers against this doctrine. Much of the argumentation in the last three chapters of Book I of the *Institutes* is concerned with it. It is of interest that the last work in which Calvin was engaged before his work was arrested by the hand of death was his exposition of the prophecy of Ezekiel. His work ended with Ezekiel 20:44. He did not even complete his exposition of the chapter. At Ezekiel 18:23, in dealing with the discrepancy between God's will to the salvation of all and the election of God by which he predestinates only a fixed number to salvation, he says: "If any one again objects—this is making God act with duplicity, the answer is ready, that God always wishes the same thing, though by different ways, and in a manner inscrutable to us. Although, therefore, God's will is simple, yet great variety is involved in it, as far as our senses are concerned. Besides, it is not surprising that our eyes should be blinded by intense light, so that we cannot certainly judge how God wishes all to be saved, and yet has devoted all the reprobate to eternal destruction, and wishes them to perish. While we look now through a glass darkly, we should be content with the measure of our own intelligence."[44]

---

[44]*Comm. ad* Ezek. 18:23; E.T. by Thomas Myers. It is more probable that the Latin verb *velle,* translated on three occasions above by the English term "wishes," should rather be rendered "wills." The present writer is not persuaded that we may speak of God's will as "simple," after the pattern of Calvin's statement. There is the undeniable fact that, in regard to sin, God *decretively* wills what he *preceptively* does not will. There is the contradiction. We must maintain that it is perfectly consistent with God's perfection that this contradiction should obtain. But it does not appear to be any resolution to say that God's will is "simple," even in the sense of the Latin term *simplex.*

I said previously that in this discrepancy the doctrine of God's sovereignty comes to its most pointed expression. It is so, I submit, because the sovereignty of God bears upon us at no point more relevantly and with more irresistible sanction than in his command. Nothing underlines God's sovereignty over us and his propriety in us, as creatures made in his image, as does his sovereign command. In his command his sovereignty is addressed to our responsibility and our responsibility defines our creaturehood as made in his image. And the command of God registers his supremacy and our complete subjection to him. The providence of God, as also his decretive will, is at no point exemplified and vindicated as to its all-inclusiveness more effectively than at the point where our responsible agency is exercised in violation of his command. There is, after all, the contradiction that we by sin offer to God's sovereignty. It is the contradiction of the claim which his sovereignty demands of us and the contradiction of what is God's good pleasure. But if the providence of God did not embrace that very contradiction, then there would be a sphere outside the realm of God's providence and, therefore, outside the sphere of his sovereign control and direction. The simple upshot of that alternative would be that God would not be sovereign, and man in his sin would be able to command a realm impervious to God's providence.

What a dismal perspective and prospect that alternative would offer to us! We must boldly maintain and profess the only alternative which Calvin so insistently asserted. In the realm of sin we do have the contradiction of God's revealed and prescriptive good pleasure. But that very contradiction is embraced in the determinate counsel and foreknowledge of God. And it is just because this is the case, it is just because the contradiction which sin offers to his sovereignty in command is embraced in the sovereignty of both decree and providence and does not create a realm impervious to his efficient foreordination and operation that the sovereign provisions of his grace invade that same realm and emancipate men from the contradiction itself and therefore from the curse, condemnation, thraldom, and misery which the contradiction entails.

It is this doctrine of God's sovereignty in the realm of sin that is the precondition of sovereignty in redemptive grace.

SUBJECT
AND
SCRIPTURE
INDICES

Subject Index

Scripture Index

OTHER SOLID GROUND TITLES

We recently celebrated our eighth anniversary of uncovering buried treasure to the glory of God. During these eight years we have produced over 225 volumes. A sample is listed below:

Biblical & Theological Studies: *Addresses to Commemorate the 100th Anniversary of Princeton Theological Seminary in 1912* by Allis, Machen, Wilson, Vos, Warfield and many more.

Notes on Galatians by J. Gresham Machen

The Origin of Paul's Religion by J. Gresham Machen

A Scientific Investigation of the Old Testament by R.D. Wilson

Theology on Fire: *Sermons from Joseph A. Alexander*

Evangelical Truth: *Sermons for the Family* by Archibald Alexander

A Shepherd's Heart: *Pastoral Sermons of James W. Alexander*

Grace & Glory: *Sermons from Princeton Chapel* by Geerhardus Vos

The Lord of Glory by Benjamin B. Warfield

The Person & Work of the Holy Spirit by Benjamin B. Warfield

The Power of God unto Salvation by Benjamin B. Warfield

Calvin Memorial Addresses by Warfield, Johnson, Orr, Webb...

The Five Points of Calvinism by Robert Lewis Dabney

Annals of the American Presbyterian Pulpit by W.B. Sprague

The Word & Prayer: *Classic Devotions from the Pen of John Calvin*

A Body of Divinity: *Sum and Substance of Christian Doctrine* by Ussher

The Complete Works of Thomas Manton (in 22 volumes)

A Puritan New Testament Commentary by John Trapp

Exposition of the Epistle to the Hebrews by William Gouge

Exposition of the Epistle of Jude by William Jenkyn

Lectures on the Book of Esther by Thomas M'Crie

Lectures on the Book of Acts by John Dick

To order any of our titles please contact us in one of three ways:

Call us at **1-866-789-7423**
Email us at **sgcb@charter.net**
Visit our website at **www.solid-ground-books.com**

THE FEAR OF GOD
The Soul of Godliness
John Murray

"Many of us owe more than we can say to the example and teaching of John Murray. He wrote nothing hurriedly and for the short term. These pages, as much as anything he prepared, take us to a most vital aspect of a true relationship with God.May they help another generation to be faithful servants of Christ!." - Iain Murray, Author of "The Life of John Murray"

"Historically, and more importantly biblically, the fear of God has been regarded as essential to true devotion to God. But in recent years this foundational element of piety has been overlooked or even rejected as belonging to the era of the old covenant and not properly Christian (I actually read the latter sentiment in book by a popular North American author!) How welcome then to have John Murray's classic study of the fear of God available in this format. Read it and nourish your soul!" - Dr. Michael Haykin

"The fear of God could be nothing less than the soul of rectitude. It is the apprehension of God's glory that constrains the fear of his name. It is that same glory that commands our totality commitment to him, totality trust and obedience. The fear of God is but the reflex in our consciousness of the transcendent perfection which alone could warrant and demand the totality of our commitment in love and devotion." - Professor John Murray

Order from Solid Ground Christian Books

PRINCIPLES OF CONDUCT
Aspects of Biblical Ethics
John Murray

A modern theological classic, John Murray's *Principles of Conduct* clearly shows the organic unity and continuity of the biblical ethic. Murray here addresses ethical questions relating to such topics as marriage, labor, capital punishment, truthfulness, Jesus' teaching in the Sermon on the Mount, law and grace and the fear of God (as seen in this booklet). Though the Ten Commandments furnish the core of the biblical ethic, Murray points the reader again and again to all of Scripture as the basic and final authority in all matters of Christian conduct.

J.I. Packer wrote in the Foreword, "An inheritor of the combined wisdom of Puritanism and Princeton, Murray did his work as a trustee of the Reformed tradition. . . . His special con-tribution was to buttress and burnish this heritage through the discipline of biblical theology, practiced according to the redemptive-historical approach that the great Geerhardus Vos, one of Murray's teachers, pioneered a century ago."

ISBN: 978-0-8028-1144-8

Principles of Conduct may be purchased from Wm. B. Eerdmans Publishing Company by calling 800-253-7521, or sending an email to customerservice@eerdmans.com.

Printed in the United States
216756BV00001B/1/P